50 Mason Jar Salad Recipes

Your Ultimate Guide to Making Salad in a Jar

Disclaimer and Terms of Use:

Effort has been made to ensure that the information in this book is accurate and complete, however, the author and the publisher do not warrant the accuracy of the information, text and graphics contained within the book due to the rapidly changing nature of science, research, known and unknown facts and internet. The Author and the publisher do not hold any responsibility for errors, omissions or contrary interpretation of the subject matter herein. This book is presented solely for motivational and informational purposes only.

Table of Contents

Introduction

Mason jar salad recipes are fast becoming an internet sensation. Why? Simply because it is easy to make, healthy and over hundreds of variations of salads to choose from. It is a perfect go to meal fix by many people who live fast paced lives and yet still want to enjoy healthy food.

Mason jar salad recipes takes its name from Mason jars and then the veggies, fruits, nuts and dressing are layered in such a way that it keeps fresh and crunchy in the refrigerator even after five days. This enables busy people to set aside a day of grocery and creating fresh mason jar salads and just store them in the ref, as a pick me up meal in the coming days. And then the cycle goes again.

So, before I give you the recipes, let me give you a few quick tips in layering your Mason jar. Plus, if you want to have a salad in a jar that's good for one person, I recommend you use the 1-pint size Mason jar. If you want a full day's worth of salad in a jar then go for a quart-sized mason jar.

To layer your mason jar, you have to place your dressing as the first layer or wet fruits and vegetables like cucumbers and tomatoes. This will help contain the wetness at the bottom of the jar and not affect the crunchiness of other ingredients. The next layer would be vegetables or fruits that are resistant to moisture, as they will be right next to the wet ingredients. Great examples of these are carrots. Then the next layer is the dry ingredients like pasta and greens. If you are adding something crunchy like nuts then these are the last items to be added. Once you are ready to eat the salad, just shake, shake and shake before enjoying.

Layering is important if you are storing this salad in a jar for a few days before consuming so that you won't end up eating something mushy. But, if you are going to eat your salad right away, go ahead and dump the ingredients in.

And lastly, to ensure that your salads last long in the ref, lessen its moisture content. Meaning, you have to dry your salad greens with paper towels or spin dry them or else, they won't last long—the longest would be a day or two.

Greek Styled Chicken Mason Jar Salad

Servings: 2 1-pint Mason jars

Ingredients:
¼ cup slivered almonds
1/3 cup grapes, halved
1/3 cup apple, diced
1/3 cup celery, diced
½ cup nonfat Greek yogurt
2 large boneless, skinless chicken breasts, poached and cubed
1 tsp lemon juice
1 cup water
1 medium head Romaine lettuce, chopped

Assembly Directions:

1) If you are planning to store this salad recipe, mix water and lemon juice. Place the diced apples into the lemon water mixture for at least 5 minutes before using. This will ensure that the apples won't turn brown. After that, drain apples and discard lemon-water.
2) In a quart of Mason jar (or 2 jars of 1-pint Mason jar), place yogurt and evenly spread.
3) Place chicken breast cubes.
4) Top with apples and grapes.

5) Cover with celery, lettuce and almonds.
6) Cover jar tightly and store. Best when eaten within 3-days of preparing.

Minty Cucumber and Chickpeas Parfait

Servings: 2 1-pint Mason jars

Ingredients:
1 cup cooked chickpeas
½ cup raisins
Pepper and salt to taste
¼ cup finely chopped fresh mint
2 cups nonfat Greek yogurt
2 cups grated cucumber
2 tbsps walnuts, chopped

Assembly Directions:

1) The first step is to grate the cucumber and the most important thing here is to squeeze out the juice so that your salad won't be swimming in cucumber juice. After grating, place cucumber in a cheesecloth and squeeze out moisture. Transfer cucumber into a paper towel and continue pressing out excess juice.
2) Mix mint and yogurt. Season with pepper and salt to taste.
3) Evenly divide the ingredients into two and layer. First add seasoned yogurt, cucumber, raisins, chickpeas, and topped with walnuts. You can garnish with a sprinkle of chopped mint.

4) Cover and store for up to 5 days in the ref.

Time-Honored Greek Salad in a Jar

Servings: 1 1-quart Mason jar

Ingredients:
2 cups Romaine lettuce, chopped
1 tbsp pine nuts
¼ cup Feta cheese, crumbled
6 Kalamata olives, pitted
¼ cup chopped carrots
¼ cup chopped red onion
¼ cup chopped celery
¼ cup chopped cucumbers
3 tbsps Creamy Greek Dressing

Assembly Directions:

1) Layer Creamy Greek dressing. If using 2 1-pint Mason jars, half each ingredient and follow the same layering process.
2) Add onions, cucumbers, celery and carrots.
3) Layer on olives.
4) If you are planning to eat this salad within 24 hours of preparation then next to olives add the cheese. But if not, I suggest that you add the cheese when you are ready to eat along with the pine nuts.

5) Top with chopped lettuce, cover jar and refrigerate until ready to use. Can be stored for up to a week in the ref.

Pears and Pomegranate Salad in a Jar

Servings: 1 1-quart Mason jar

Ingredients:
3 tbsps Sherry Vinaigrette
2 oz crumbled blue cheese
¼ cup roughly chopped pecans
½ cup pomegranate seeds
3 cups spinach leaves, divided
1 pear, cored and thinly sliced
1 tsp lemon juice + 1 cup water

Sherry Vinaigrette Ingredients:
3 tbsps olive oil
Freshly ground black pepper, to taste
A pinch of salt
2 ½ tbsps sherry vinegar

Assembly Directions:

1) Mix water and lemon juice. Immerse sliced pear into juice for at least 5 minutes. This will protect pears from browning. Once done, drain and discard lemon water. Pat pears dry with paper towel.
2) Layer pears on bottom of jar.
3) Layer 2 cups of spinach on top of pears, followed by pomegranate seeds.

4) Add another ½ cup of spinach, top with pecans and cover with remaining spinach.
5) Meanwhile in a small bowl mix sherry vinaigrette ingredients. Then transfer 3 tbsps of mixture into a small and lidded cup.
6) If storing this salad for a couple of days, just place the lidded cup of vinaigrette inside the jar and just add the cheese when ready to eat.
7) Cover jar and store in the ref for up to 5 days.

Tortellini, Spinach and Arugula Salad

Servings: 5 1-quart Mason jars

Ingredients:
5 cups spinach and arugula blend
5 oz goat cheese
4 oz dried cheese filled tortellini, cook according to package instructions
2 cans quartered artichoke hearts, cut in half
1 red onion, chopped
1 quart cherry tomatoes, halved
10 tbsps Italian dressing of choice

Assembly Directions:

1) Evenly divide ingredients into 5.
2) Layer according to the following: dressing, onions and tomatoes. Then followed by chopped artichokes, top with tortellini, goat cheese and cover with spinach-arugula blend.
3) Cover jar and store in the ref. Best when consumed within 2 to 3 days of preparation.

Spinach-Avocado Dressing on Zucchini Noodle Salad

Servings: 2 1-pint Mason jars

Ingredients:

2 tbsps Kalamata olives

¼ cup feta cheese

½ cup cherry tomatoes

½ cup sliced celery

½ cup shelled edamame

1 ½ cups spiraled zucchini noodles

Spinach-Avocado Dressing Ingredients:

¼ tsp pepper

½ tsp salt

2 tbsps nonfat plain Greek yogurt

2 tbsps extra virgin olive oil

Juice of 1 lemon

½ ripe avocado

½ cup fresh packed spinach

Assembly Directions:

1) Spiralize zucchini or shred into noodle like pieces. And set aside.

2) In a blender, blend all dressing ingredients until smooth and creamy. When done, evenly divide in bottom of each Mason jar.
3) Divide ingredients into two and layer on: celery, edamame, feta cheese, tomatoes, olives and zucchini noodles.
4) Cover and refrigerate. Lasts up to 5 days in the ref.

Asparagus, Quinoa and Zucchini Noodle Salad

Servings: 1 1-pint Mason jar

Ingredients:
¼ cup cubed feta
2-3 stalks scallion, diced
1 medium zucchini, spiralized
¼ cup green peas
3 asparagus stalks, chopped into 1-inch piece
1 ½ tsp coconut flakes
2 tsps minced cilantro
1/3 cup cooked quinoa

Dressing Ingredients:
juice of ½ lime
2 tbsps coconut milk
½ avocado

Assembly Directions:

1) To make the dressing, combine all ingredients in a food processor and process until smooth and creamy. Pour into bottom of jar.
2) Fill a small saucepan halfway with water and bring to a boil. Once boiling, lower fire to a simmer and blanch asparagus. After a minute add peas and

continue cooking until tender, around 4minutes while covered. Drain veggies and allow to cool.

3) In bowl, mix coconut flakes, cilantro and quinoa. Toss to coat well.

4) To assemble salad in a jar, layer on top of dressing the zucchini noodles, quinoa mixture, scallions, peas and asparagus. Drizzle with feta.

5) Cover and store in the ref for up to 3 days.

Caprese Mason Jar Salad

Servings: 1 1-pint Mason jar

Ingredients:
1 small Bocconcini cheese, sliced
½ cup cherry tomatoes, halved
½ cup purple basil leaves
½ cup green basil leaves
2 cups arugula

Dressing Ingredients:
Black pepper and salt to taste
a drop of honey
½ tbsp balsamic vinegar
2 tbsps extra virgin olive oil

Assembly Directions:

1) In a pint of salad jar, layer arugula, purple basil, green basil, bocconcini and tomatoes.
2) If planning to eat later, cover and store salad in the ref. Best if used within 5 days of preparation.
3) To eat, mix dressing ingredients in a small bowl and drizzle over salad. Cover, shake jar to mix well, uncover and enjoy.

Strawberry Vinaigrette Dressed Chicken-Beet Salad

Servings: 1 1-pint Mason jar

Ingredients:
5 pecans, chopped
1 oz goat cheese
2 cups raw spinach
½ apple, washed and diced
3 oz raw chicken breast
Pepper and salt to taste
1 tsp olive oil
2 beets scrubbed
1 tsp lemon juice + 1 cup water

Dressing Ingredients:
¼ tsp honey
Pinch of dried tarragon
Pepper and salt to taste
½ tbsp balsamic vinegar
½ tbsp olive oil
¼ cup strawberries

Assembly Directions:

1) Mix lemon juice and water in a medium bowl and submerge diced apple for 5 minutes. When done, drain and discard lemon water.

2) In a blender, puree dressing by combining all ingredients in a food processor. Once smooth, pour into jar.

3) Preheat grill to medium fire. Wash, peel and slice beets. Place beets in a bowl and drizzle with ½ tsp olive oil. Toss to coat well. Grill beets until tender, around 5 minutes per side. Once cooked, slice beets in half once more.

4) Pound chicken breasts to attain a uniform thickness. Drizzle with remaining olive oil and season with pepper and salt. Grill until juices run clear, around 5 minutes per side. Remove from grill and allow to cool for at least 15 minutes. Once cool to touch, dice grilled chicken to ½-inch cubes and continue to cool for another 10 minutes.

5) To layer salad, add in the following order: beets, spinach, apples, chicken, goat cheese and pecans.

6) Cover and refrigerate until ready to eat.

Vegan Cobb Salad in a Jar

Servings: 1 1-pint Mason jar

Ingredients:
¼ cup extra firm tofu, diced
¼ avocado fruit, diced
½ Navel orange, peeled and separated into sections
1 medium tomato, diced
½ medium onion, diced
1 medium carrot, peeled and diced
1 cup arugula
¼ cup smoked ham, diced
1 cup Romaine lettuce, chopped

Dressing Ingredients:
¼ tsp pepper
¼ tsp salt
1 small clove garlic, peeled and minced
1 tsp Worcestershire sauce
1 tsp Dijon mustard
1 tbsp lemon juice
2 tbsps red wine vinegar
3 tbsps olive oil

Assembly Directions:

1) In a food processor, process all dressing ingredients until smooth and creamy. Add 2 tbsps of dressing into a pint of Mason jar. Keep remaining dressing for future use.
2) To assemble, add the following in order: tomatoes, onion, oranges, avocado, carrots, ham, tofu, arugula, and lettuce.
3) Cover and store in the ref until ready to use.

Green Salad With Cajun Shrimp

Servings: 1 1-pint Mason jar

Ingredients:
Salt to taste
½ tsp Cajun seasoning
3 large shrimps, peeled and deveined
1 ½ tbsps olive oil
½ green bell pepper, chopped
½ red bell pepper, chopped
1 medium onion, sliced
¼ cup guacamole
2 cups Spinach

Assembly Directions:

1) On medium high fire, place a nonstick small fry pan and heat ½ tbsp oil. Once hot, sauté red and green peppers until soft, around 5 minutes. Transfer to bottom of Mason jar. On same pan, add another ½ tbsp oil and sauté onions until starting to be translucent on the edges, around 3 to 5 minutes. Transfer onion on top of sautéed bell peppers.
2) Meanwhile, season shrimps with salt and Cajun seasoning. On same fry pan add remaining oil and stir fry shrimps until opaque. Transfer on top of

onions. Allow to cool before adding remaining salad ingredients, around 20 to 30 minutes.

3) Cover shrimps with guacamole and spinach.
4) Cover and refrigerate until ready to eat. Best if eaten within 5 days of preparation.

Taco Salad In a Jar

Servings: 1 1-pint Mason jar

Ingredients:
1 tsp taco seasoning
¼ cup ground beef
1 tsp olive oil
1 stalk scallions, chopped
2 cups packed lettuce, shredded
½ cup salsa
½ red onion, diced
1 medium tomato, diced
2 tbsps Pepper Jack cheese, shredded

Assembly Directions:

1) On medium high fire, place small nonstick saucepan and heat oil. Once oil is hot, sauté beef. Add taco seasoning and sauté until cooked, around 5 to 8 minutes. Add pepper if desired. Allow to cool completely.
2) In Mason jar, place salsa, tomato and onions.
3) Top with cooled and cooked ground beef. Cover with shredded lettuce and chopped scallions.
4) Cover and refrigerate until ready to eat.
5) When ready to eat, sprinkle cheese on top and enjoy.

Antipasto with Chicken pesto salad

Servings: 1 1-pint Mason jar

Ingredients:
1 tbsp pesto
1 chicken breast, cut into ½ inch cubes
1 red pepper, roasted and chopped
1 medium tomato, chopped
½ red onion, chopped
4 Pepperoni slices, quartered
4 tbsps extra virgin olive oil, divided
2 tbsps fresh mozzarella cheese, cubed
1 cup packed spinach
salt to taste

Assembly Directions:

1) On medium high fire, place a small nonstick pan and heat ½ tbsp olive oil. Add chicken and pesto, sauté until chicken is cooked. Season with salt to taste. Allow to cool completely.
2) In Mason jar, assemble in the following order: tomatoes, onions, roasted red peppers, mozzarella, chicken-pesto (scrape pan), pepperoni and spinach.
3) Drizzle remaining olive oil into jar, cover and store for up to 5 days.

Mediterranean Styled Salad

Servings: 1 1-pint Mason jar

Ingredients:
2 tbsps lemon vinaigrette
½ medium cucumber, scrubbed clean and diced with skin on
1 medium tomato, diced
½ red onion, diced
2 artichoke hearts, quartered
½ cup feta cheese, cubed
2 cups spinach

Lemon Vinaigrette Ingredients:
Salt to taste
1 tbsp raw honey
Juice of 1 lemon
1 tbsp minced garlic
½ cup rice vinegar
¼ cup extra virgin olive oil

Assembly Directions:

1) To make the dressing, combine all ingredients in a small and lidded jar. Shake well before each use. Scoop out 2 tbsps of the dressing and add to a pint of Mason jar.

2) To assemble salad, layer on in order: cucumbers, tomatoes, onions, artichokes, feta cheese, and spinach.

3) Cover and store in the ref for 5 to 7 days.

Fava Beans and Stone Fruit Salad

Servings: 1 1-pint Mason jar

Ingredients:
A pinch of salt
1 garlic clove, minced
1 tsp virgin coconut oil
25 pieces of whole fava beans, removed from pods and leathery skin peeled off
2 cups arugula and matché lettuce mix
1 nectarine, pitted and sliced
2 apricots, pitted and sliced
½ avocado, pitted and peeled
¼ cup pistachios, shelled raw and unsalted
1 small cucumber, julienned

Minty Lime Dressing Ingredients:
1 spring onion, and chop finely
1 ½ tbsps virgin coconut oil
Juice of 1 lime and zest
1 small handful of mint leaves

Assembly Directions:

1) In a food processor, process all dressing ingredients until well combined. Pour into bottom of Mason

jar, if planning to eat right away. If not, just add the dressing when ready to eat.

2) On medium fire, place a nonstick fry pan and heat coconut oil. Sauté garlic until lightly browned. Add fava beans and season with pepper and salt. Continue sautéing for a minute or two. Turn off fire and allow to cool completely.

3) To layer the salad, just add the following in sequence: cucumber, cooled fava beans (include the garlic and oil), nectarines, avocado, apricots, pistachios, and greens.

4) Cover and store in the ref for up to 3 days.

Corn and Black Bean Salad

Servings: 5 1-quart Mason jars

Ingredients:
¼ cup or more chopped cilantro – optional
5 cups chopped Romaine lettuce
5 oz block of pepper jack cheese, cut into small cubes
2 avocados, peeled, pitted and chopped
1 12-oz package frozen corn, thawed
2 cans black beans, drained and rinsed
1 red onion, chopped
1 quart cherry tomatoes, halved
1 6-oz container nonfat plain Greek yogurt
1 ¼ cup salsa

Assembly Directions:

1) To assemble salad, just layer the following ingredients in order per jar: ¼ cup salsa, 1/5 of Greek yogurt, ½ of tomatoes, ½ of red onion, 1/5 of black beans, 1/5 of corn, 1/5 of avocado, 1/5 of cheese, 1 cup lettuce and 1/5 of cilantro.
2) Cover and store in the ref for up to 5 days.

Noodle Salad Asian Style

Servings: 4 1-pint Mason jars

Ingredients:
½ cup crunchy rice noodles
4 green onions, thinly sliced
2 large carrots, peeled and shredded
1 cup shelled edamame, cooked
1 red bell pepper, thinly sliced
4 oz soba noodles

Spicy Peanut Dressing:
1 tbsp black sesame seeds
¼ cup extra virgin olive oil
4 tsps soy sauce
4 tsps rice vinegar
4 tsps sambal oelek
2 tbsps peanut butter

Assembly Directions:

1) cook noodles in a large boiling pot of water following manufacturer's instructions. Once cooked, drain and rinse in cold water.
2) To make the dressing, in a food processor, combine all ingredients except for sesame seeds. Puree until smooth and creamy. Stir in sesame seeds.

3) In a bowl, mix dressing and soba noodles until thoroughly coated. Divide into 4.
4) To assemble salad, layer in sequence the following: soba noodles with dressing, bell pepper, edamame, carrots, green onions and crunchy rice noodles.
5) Cover and refrigerate until ready to eat. Best served within 5 days of preparation.

Lime and Cilantro Dressing on Taco Salad

Servings: 1 1-quart Mason jar

Ingredients:
1 tbsp shredded cheddar cheese
¼ avocado, diced
3 cups iceberg lettuce shredded
¼ cup red pepper, diced
¼ cup corn
1 roma tomato, diced
½ cup black beans
¼ cucumber, diced

Lime-Cilantro Dressing:
A pinch of salt
1 tsp honey
¼ cup nonfat plain Greek yogurt
½ cup fresh cilantro, loosely packed
Juice of 1 lime
1 tbsp apple cider vinegar

Assembly Directions:

1) In food processor, process all dressing ingredients until smooth and creamy. Pour into bottom of Mason jar.

2) Layer salad ingredients as follows: cucumbers, black beans, tomato, corn, red pepper, iceberg lettuce, avocado and cheese.
3) Cover and refrigerate until ready to eat. Best served within 3 days of preparation. Great wide a side of toasted taco shell.

Orzo and Spinach Salad

Servings: 4 1-quart Mason jars

Ingredients:
5 oz baby spinach
8 oz fresh ciliegine mozzarella balls
1 cup halved snap peas
1 pint cherry tomatoes cut in half
½ tsp pepper
½ tsp salt
½ cup chopped fresh herbs
1 tbsp fresh lemon juice
2 tsps grated lemon zest
3 tbsps olive oil
1 cup orzo

Assembly Directions:

1) Following manufacturer's instructions, cook orzo.
2) In a bowl, mix pepper, salt, herbs, lemon juice, lemon zest and oil thoroughly. Evenly divide into four and pour into each jar.
3) To assemble salad, layer in the following order: ¼ of tomatoes, ¼ of cooked orzo, ¼ of snap peas, ¼ of mozzarella, and ¼ of spinach.
4) Cover and store until ready to eat. Best served within 4 days of preparation.

Cranberry and Garden Salad Mix

Servings: 1 1-quart Mason jar

Ingredients:
2 cups Spring Mix Salad greens
1 cup arugula
1 large egg, boiled, peeled and sliced
1 tbsp craisins
¼ cup frozen corn, thawed and drained well
4 slices of beets, cooked and drained well
1 tbsp Parmesan cheese
1 tsp lemon juice
3 tsps extra virgin olive oil
1 tsp honey

Assembly Directions:

1) In a small bowl, mix honey, olive oil and lemon juice to make the dressing. Once thoroughly mixed, pour into Mason jar.
2) To layer, place the ingredients in the following order: beets, corn, egg, craisins, arugula and spring mix.
3) Cover and refrigerate for up to 2 days.

Ginger-Orange Dressing on Quinoa Salad

Servings: 4 1-pint Mason jars

Ingredients:
Salt to taste
½ cup finely chopped fresh parsley
1 ½ cups diced green pepper
1 ½ cups diced red pepper
1 cup diced carrots
1 cup edamame
1 cup uncooked quinoa
1 cup uncooked wheatberries

Dressing Ingredients:
Salt to taste
1 tbsp fresh lime juice
1 tbsp fresh minced ginger
1 tbsp apple cider vinegar
1/3 cup 100% pure apple juice
2/3 cup 100% pure orange juice

Assembly Directions:

1) Thoroughly wash quinoa to remove saponins which create a bitter taste. To cook quinoa, place in pot with 1 ½ cups water and bring to a boil. Once boiling, lower fir to a simmer, cover and cook for

15-20 minutes or until all water is fully absorbed and quinoa is light and fluffy. Allow to cool completely.

2) Cook wheatberries just like quinoa but use 2 cups water and cook for 5 minutes longer. Wheatberries should be tender yet chewy. Allow to cool completely.

3) To make the dressing, combine all ingredients in a bowl and whisk to mix well. Divide into four and pour into Mason jars.

4) To layer salad, add the following ingredients in sequence: ½ cup wheatberries, ¼ cup red pepper, ¼ cup green pepper, ½ cup quinoa, ½ cup carrots, 2 tbsps parsley, and ¼ cup edamame.

5) Cover and refrigerate until ready to eat. Best eaten within 6 days of preparation.

Blue Cheese, Blueberry and Spinach Salad

Servings: 1 1-quart Mason jar

Ingredients:
3 tbsps Red Wine Vinaigrette
2 oz crumbled blue cheese
¼ cup sliced almonds
3 cups spinach leaves, divided
½ cup blueberries

Assembly Directions:

1) To layer salad, add ingredients in the following order: blueberries, 2 cups spinach, almonds, rest of spinach, and blue cheese.
2) Cover and refrigerate for up to 5 days.
3) When ready to eat, that's the time to pour in the red vine vinaigrette dressing.

Lime-Strawberry Vinaigrette on Spinach Salad

Servings: 1 1-pint Mason jar

Ingredients:
1 cup baby spinach
1 tbsp crumbled Feta
1 stalk sliced green onions
1 tsp sunflower seeds
½ cup sliced strawberries
½ cup cooked quinoa
2 tbsps lime-strawberry vinaigrette

Lime Strawberry Vinaigrette Ingredients:
Pepper and salt to taste
1 tbsp white wine vinegar
1 tsp mustard
1 tbsps fresh lime juice
2 tsps strawberry preserves
2 tbsps extra virgin olive oil

Assembly Directions:

1) To make the dressing, add all ingredients in a food processor and puree until smooth and creamy. Scoop out 2 tbsps of the dressing and pour into Mason jar. Store remaining dressing for future use.

2) To assemble salad, layer ingredients in the following sequence: quinoa, strawberries, sunflower seeds, green onions, feta cheese and baby spinach.
3) Cover and store in the ref for until 5 days.

Crunchy and Orange-y Salad

Servings: 1 1-pint Mason jar

Ingredients:
1 cup Baby spinach
1 cup Romaine lettuce, chopped
1 tbsp pine nuts
¼ cup sprouted lentils
½ red onion, sliced
2 clementine, peeled and separated into sections
½ cup cooked quinoa
2 tbsps Orange Marmalade Vinaigrette

Orange Marmalade Vinaigrette Ingredients:
Pepper and salt to taste
Pinch of red pepper flakes
2 tsps extra virgin olive oil
2 tbsps apple cider vinegar
2 tsps orange marmalade

Assembly Directions:

1) In food processor, combine all vinaigrette ingredients and puree until smooth and creamy. Scoop out 2 tbsps of the dressing and pour into Mason jar. Store and refrigerate remaining dressing for future use.

2) To assemble salad in a jar, layer the following in sequence: cooked quinoa, clementine sections, sprouted lentils, pine nuts, chopped romaine and baby spinach.

3) Cover and refrigerate for up to 5 days.

Lemon and Sesame Dressing on Tofu Salad

Servings: 1 1-pint Mason jar

Ingredients:
1 cup chopped Romaine
1 tbsp chopped parsley
1 tsp sunflower seeds
½ cup sprouted lentils
1 medium cucumbers, scrubbed and chopped with skin on
½ red bell pepper, sliced
½ package of extra firm tofu, drained, pressed and sliced into ½-inch cubes

Lemon Sesame Dressing Ingredients:
1 clove garlic, minced
¼ tsp oregano
¼ tsp black pepper
¼ tsp salt
1 tsp honey
1 tbsp rice wine vinegar
1 tsp sesame oil
A pinch of red pepper flakes
1 tbsp lemon juice
1 tbsp tahini

Assembly Directions:

1) In a food processor, combine all dressing ingredients and puree until smooth and creamy. Scoop out 2tbsps of dressing and pour into Mason jar. Transfer to a lidded container the remaining dressing and store for future use.
2) To assemble salad in a jar, layer the following in sequence: cubed tofu, bell pepper, cucumbers, lentils, sunflower seeds, chopped parsley and Romaine lettuce.
3) Cover and store for up to 2 days from preparation.

Lime and Chile Dressing on Mexican Style Salad

Servings: 1 1-pint Mason jar

Ingredients:
1 cup packed chopped Romaine
1 tbsp chopped cilantro
½ cup haled grape tomatoes
½ medium red onions, sliced
½ cup salsa
½ cup cooked chickpeas
¼ cup cooked brown rice

Lime-Chile Dressing Ingredients:
Pepper and salt to taste
A pinch of red pepper flakes
1 tsp dried ground cumin
2 tbsps fresh lime juice
2 tbsps extra virgin olive oil

Assembly Directions:

1) Add all dressing ingredients in a food processor and process until smooth and creamy/. Adjust pepper and salt to taste then mix well. Scoop out 2 tbsps of dressing and pour into Mason jar. Store remaining dressing for future use.

2) To assemble salad in a jar, layer the following in order: Brown rice, chickpeas, salsa, red onions, grape tomatoes, cilantro, and romaine lettuce.

3) Cover and store in the ref for no more than 2 days.

Creamy Orzo and Citrus Chicken Salad

Servings: 2 1-pint Mason jars

Ingredients:
2 cups fresh spinach
1 cup red onion, chopped finely
2 whole roasted red peppers, diced
1 chicken breast, grilled or poached, shredded
2 cup orzo, cooked according to manufacturer's instructions

Creamy Citrus Dressing Ingredients:
Pepper and salt to taste
2 tbsps olive oil
1 tsp balsamic vinegar
1 ½ tsps orange zest
¼ cup orange juice
2 tbsps Greek yogurt

Assembly Directions:

1) In food processor, process all dressing ingredients until smooth and creamy. Divide into two and pour into two Mason jars.
2) To assemble salad in a jar, evenly divide ingredients into two and layer in the following order: roasted

red peppers, red onions, orzo, shredded chicken and spinach.

3) Cover and refrigerate for no more than 5 days.

Balsamic Vinaigrette Dresses Quinoa and Roasted Sweet Potato Salad

Servings: 1 1-quart Mason jar

Ingredients:
1 tbsp salted sunflower seeds
1 tbsp dried cranberries
2 cups spring mix salad greens
¼ red pepper, diced
½ cup black beans
¼ cup quinoa
Pepper and salt to taste
1 tbsp olive oil
1 small sweet potato, unpeeled, diced into bite sized pieces

Dressing Ingredients:
1 ½ tbsps water
1 tbsp balsamic vinegar
¼ cup mango

Assembly Directions:

1) Preheat oven to 400°F. Place potatoes in a baking pan. Season with pepper and salt. Drizzle with oil. Toss potatoes to coat well with oil and seasoning. Place in the oven and roast until soft, around 20

minutes. After the first ten minutes of roasting, remove potatoes and stir to cook evenly before returning into oven. Once cooked, cool completely

2) Meanwhile, bring quinoa and ½ cup of water to a boil in a small pot. Once boiling, lower fire to a simmer, cover and cook until liquid is fully absorbed and quinoa is tender and fluffy, around 15-20 minutes. Once cooked, cool completely.

3) In food processor, mix all dressing ingredients and puree until smooth and creamy.

4) To layer salad in a jar, add the following in order: black beans, quinoa, and dressing. Stir to mix well.

5) Add in sequence: red pepper, greens, sweet potatoes, sunflower seeds and cranberries.

6) Cover and refrigerate until ready to use. Store for no more than 3 days.

Thyme and Mustard Vinaigrette on Spinach & Chicken Salad

Servings: 4 1-pint Mason jars

Ingredients:
4 cups baby spinach, torn roughly
1/3 cup shaved Asiago cheese
1/3 cup walnuts, roughly chopped
2 cups red grapes, halved
8oz cooked chicken breast, chopped roughly

Thyme-Mustard Vinaigrette Ingredients:
5 tbsps extra virgin olive oil
¼ tsp freshly ground black pepper
¼ tsp salt
¾ chopped fresh thyme leaves
5 tsps Dijon mustard
5 tsps red wine vinegar

Assembly Directions:

1) In a food processor, add all vinaigrette ingredients and puree until smooth and creamy. Divide into four and pour into corresponding jars.
2) To make salad in a jar, layer the following in sequence: chicken, grapes, walnuts, cheese and spinach.

3) Cover and refrigerate for no more than 3 days.

Beet Vinaigrette on Quinoa Salad

Servings: 4 1-pint Mason jars

Ingredients:
Zest from 2 oranges, divided
4 tbsps chopped walnuts or pecans, or both
4 cups packed baby spinach
Salt to taste
1 tbsps coconut oil
1 tbsp fresh orange juice
1 bunch beets, cleaned, peeled and chopped into quarters
2 cups cooked quinoa

Beet Vinaigrette Ingredients:
¼ cup Avocado oil
1 tbsp unsweetened coconut milk
1 tsp lemon juice
1 ½ oz Orange juice
4 quarters of citrus coconut Roasted beet (recipe to follow)

Assembly Directions:

1) Make the coconut Roasted citrus beet by preheating oven to 400oF. In baking pan place quartered beets, season with salt, add orange juice and coconut oil. Toss to coat well. Roast for 20

minutes, remove from oven, flip beets, return to oven and continue roasting for another 20 minutes. Remove beets from oven, garnish with zest of 1 orange and allow to cool completely.

2) To make the vinaigrette, from the roasted beet above, get 4 quarters and add into a food processor. Add remaining vinaigrette ingredients and puree until smooth and creamy. Evenly divide dressing into four jars.

3) Add ½ of cooked quinoa into each jar of beet and mix well.

4) To layer remaining salad ingredients, add in order: ¼ of roasted beets, ¼ of spinach, ¼ of nuts, and ¼ of 1 orange zest.

5) Cover and refrigerate for up to 5 days.

Wild Rice, Pear and Sweet Potato Salad

Servings: 2 1-pint Mason jars

Ingredients:
2 tbsps aged white cheddar, cubed
1 red onion, diced
2 tbsps pecans, toasted and chopped
1 cup cooked wild rice, cooled
Pepper and salt to taste
1 tbsp coconut oil
1 large sweet potato, peeled and cut into ½-inch cubes
2 cups arugula

Yogurt and Honey Dressing:
Pepper and salt to taste
1 tbsp finely chopped chives
Juice from 1 large lemon
3 tbsps honey
¾ cup plain yogurt

Assembly Directions:

1) Preheat oven to 400oF. In a baking pan place cubed sweet potatoes. Season with pepper and salt. Drizzle with coconut oil and pop in the oven. Roast for 20 minutes, remove from oven, flip potatoes, return to oven and continue baking for another 15-

20 minutes. Once crisp and tender, remove from oven and cool completely.

2) In Food processor, combine all ingredients except for chives and puree until smooth and creamy. Adjust pepper and salt to taste. Add chives and mix well. Evenly divide into two mason jars.

3) To assemble salad in a jar, divide into remaining ingredients and layer in the following order: wild rice, sweet potato, pear, red onion, cheddar, pecans and arugula.

4) Cover and refrigerate up to 4 days.

Taco Salad in a Jar Version #2

Servings: 5 1-quart Mason jars

Ingredients:
5 cups chopped Romaine lettuce
11 oz jar pickled jalapeños, drained and chopped
Juice from half a lime
2 avocados, chopped
1 medium red onion, chopped
5 mini cucumbers, sliced
1 quart cherry tomatoes, halved
5 tbsps plain Greek yogurt
1 ¼ cups salsa
1 packet taco seasoning
1 can black beans, drained
1 lb ground turkey
1 tsp oil

Assembly Directions:

1) On medium high fire, place a medium nonstick fry pan and heat oil. Once hot fry ground turkey until cooked, around 5 to 8 minutes. Add seasoning packet (and water according to seasoning packet instructions) and black beans. Stir well and continue cooking for another 3 minutes. Turn off fire and allow to cool completely.

2) To arrange salad, divide ingredients into 5 servings and layer in this sequence: salsa, Greek yogurt, tomatoes, cucumbers, onions, jalapeños, avocados, turkey meat and lettuce.

3) Cover and store in the ref for no more than 5 days.

Spring Salad and Sprouts with Basil Vinaigrette

Servings: 2 1-pint Mason jars

Ingredients:
1 cup packed fresh spring sprouts of choice (onion, clover, mustard or alfalfa)
½ cup pine nuts
1 cup shelled edamame beans
1 cup cherry tomatoes
½ cup grated carrots
1 cup cooked chickpea, rinsed and drained thoroughly

Basil Vinaigrette Ingredients:
Pepper and salt to taste
1 heaping tsp of Dijon mustard
6 fresh basil leaves, chopped
2 ½ tbsps red wine vinegar
5 tbsps olive oil

Assembly Directions:

1) In food processor, combine all vinaigrette dressing and puree until smooth and creamy. Evenly divide and pour into two Mason jars.

2) To assemble salad, divide ingredients in half and layer in the following sequence: chickpea, carrots, tomato, edamame, nuts and sprouted greens.
3) Cover and refrigerate for up to 5 days.

Cajun Spiced Quinoa Salad

Servings: 1 1-pint Mason jar

Ingredients:
1 tbsp walnuts, chopped
½ cup kale, chopped
1 small carrot, peeled and julienned
½ cup cooked quinoa
1 tsp Cajun seasoning
½ red onion, chopped
1 tbsp extra virgin olive oil
1 tbsp balsamic vinegar
1 garlic clove minced
1 tsp dried Italian spices

Assembly Directions:

1) In Mason jar, allow dressing to steep in spices. So, mix balsamic vinegar, extra virgin olive oil (EVOO), garlic clove and Italian spices. Allow to sit for at least 30 minutes.
2) Meanwhile, cook quinoa according to manufacturer's instructions. Once cooked, mix in Cajun seasoning and fluff to mix well. Allow to cool completely.
3) To assemble salad, layer ingredients in the following sequence: balsamic vinegar dressing, red

onion, Cajun spiced quinoa, carrots, walnuts and kale.

4) Cover and refrigerate for no more than 5 days.

Apricots, Quinoa and Baby Chard Salad

Servings: 1 1-pint Mason jar

Ingredients:
2 tbsps diced dried apricots
1 tsp Cajun seasoning
½ cup cooked quinoa
2 tbsps walnuts, chopped
1 cup arugula
1 cup baby chard, chopped
½ cup cooked butter bean
½ sweet Maui onion, diced
1 ½ tbsps EVOO
½ tbsp lemon juice
½ tbsp honey

Assembly Directions:

1) In Mason jar mix well EVOO, lemon juice and honey. Let it stand.
2) Meanwhile, mix quinoa with Cajun seasoning and set aside.
3) To assemble salad in a jar, layer ingredients in this sequence: dressing, onions, quinoa, butter bean, dried apricots, walnuts, baby chard and arugula.
4) Cover and refrigerate for no more than 5 days.

Beans Salad Mediterranean Style

Servings: 4 1-pint Mason jars

Ingredients:
1 cup tomato, diced
1 cup cucumber, diced
1 cup feta cheese, crumbled
1 cup canned black beans, drained and rinsed well
1 cup cannellini beans canned, drained and rinsed well
2 cups garbanzo beans canned, drained and rinsed well
1 cup Israeli couscous, cooked following manufacturer's directions

Lemon-Garlic Dressing Ingredients:
Pepper and salt to taste
2 tbsps olive oil
1 whole garlic clove, minced
2 tbsps shallots finely chopped
2 whole lemon, zested and juiced

Assembly Directions:

1) In a medium bowl, mix all dressing ingredients and set aside.
2) To assemble salad in a jar, divide all ingredients into 4 equal parts and layer according to this order: dressing, cucumber, garbanzo beans, tomatoes,

cannellini beans, black beans, couscous, and feta cheese.

3) Cover and refrigerate for up to 6 days.

Another Greek Style Salad

Servings: 5 1-quart Mason jars

Ingredients:
5 cups chopped Romaine lettuce
2 cups shredded rotisserie chicken
¾ cup crumbled feta cheese
1 cup pitted Greek olives, chopped
5 mini cucumbers, sliced
1 quart cherry tomatoes, halved
10 tbsps Newman's Own Olive Oil and Vinegar Dressing

Assembly Directions:

1) To assemble salad in a jar, divide all ingredients into 5 equal servings and layer in the following order: dressing, tomatoes, cucumbers, olives, cheese, chicken and Romaine lettuce.
2) Cover and store in the refrigerator for up to 5 days.

Lime-Honey Vinaigrette on Black Bean and Mango Salad

Servings: 5 1-quart Mason jars

Ingredients:
5 cups shredded Romaine lettuce
1 cup cooked quinoa
1 can yellow corn, drained
2 cans black beans, drained
½ cup finely chopped cilantro
½ medium red onion, finely chopped
1 jalapeño, seeded and finely chopped
2 cups frozen diced mango thawed
Juice of 1 lime
2 avocados, diced

Lime-Honey Vinaigrette Ingredients:
½ cup EVOO
Pepper and salt to taste
½ tsp cumin
1 tsp garlic powder
1 tbsp Dijon mustard
1 tsp white sugar
2 tbsps honey
juice of 2 limes

Assembly Directions:

1) In food processor, blend all ingredients until smooth and creamy, around 5 minutes.
2) In two bowls, place mango and avocado. Squeeze ½ lemon juice on each bowl and toss to coat well. Season avocado with a pinch of salt and toss to mix.
3) Evenly divide all ingredients in to 5 equal servings and layer inside the jar in the following order: vinaigrette, quinoa, mango, black beans, corn, avocado, onions, jalapeño, cilantro and lettuce.
4) Cover and refrigerate up to 3 days.

Burrito in a Jar

Servings: 5 1-pint Mason jars

Ingredients:
½ + ¼ cup chopped fresh cilantro, divided
¾ cup shredded cheese
5 tbsps Greek yogurt
3 cups chopped lettuce
1 large sweet potato, washed, ends cut
bacon residual oil
2 pieces tick cut bacon
1 tbsp ghee
2 + ½ tsps sea salt, divided
2 large chicken breasts
1 lime, zested and juiced
2 cups water
1 cup quinoa

Assembly Directions:

1) Bring ½ tsp salt, water and quinoa to a boil. Once boiling, reduce fire to a simmer, cover and cook until water is fully absorbed and quinoa is tender around 20-25 minutes. Turn off fire and cool quinoa completely. Once cooled, add cilantro, lime zest and juice. Toss to mix well.
2) With paper towels, dry chicken and season with 2 tsps salt. On medium high fire, place nonstick

skillet and heat ghee. Pan fry chicken for 4 minutes per side or until cooked and juices run clear. Transfer cooked chicken to cutting board and allow to cool completely. When cooled, cut into ½-inch cubes.

3) In same pan, cook bacon until crispy. Once bacon is cooled, crumble and set aside.

4) Continue heating bacon fat on high fire and add sweet potatoes. Sear all sides of potatoes, around 3 to 5 minutes of cooking. After searing, lower fire to medium low, cover and cook potatoes for another 10 minutes or until tender. Once cooked, allow to cool completely.

5) To assemble salad in a jar, evenly divide all ingredients into 5 servings and layer ingredients in the following sequence: Greek yogurt, potato cubes, quinoa, cheese, bacon, chicken and lettuce.

6) Cover jar and refrigerate. Eat within 5 days of preparation.

Feta & Shrimp Cobb Salad

Servings: 1 1-quart Mason jar

Ingredients:
2 slices cooked bacon, chopped
1 boiled egg, sliced
6 pieces shrimp, peeled, deveined and cooked
2 tbsps chopped feta cheese
1 cup romaine lettuce chopped
1 cup baby spinach
2 tbsps chopped cucumber
1 tbsp red onion, chopped
8 grape tomatoes
2 tbsps chopped avocado
2 tbsps dressing of choice

Assembly Directions:

1) To assemble salad in a jar, layer ingredients in the following order: dressing, avocado, tomatoes, red onion, cucumber, shrimp, bacon, egg, lettuce, feta cheese, and baby spinach.
2) Cover and refrigerate for no more than 2 days.

Fruity Salad in a Jar

Servings: 4 1-pint Mason jars

Ingredients:
2 cups sliced strawberries
2 honey mango, peeled and cubed
2 tsps fresh lemon juice
2 medium bananas, sliced
2 cups watermelon sliced

Assembly Directions:

1) In a bowl, toss sliced bananas and lemon juice. This will keep bananas from turning brown.
2) Layer the fruits in this order: bananas, mangoes, watermelon and strawberries.
3) Cover and refrigerate. Consume within 2 days of preparation.

Nut and Triple Berry Salad

Servings: 4 1-pint Mason jars

Ingredients:
1 cup roasted almonds, chopped roughly
2 cup blueberries
2 cup blackberries
2 cup strawberries, hulled and quartered

Sweet Citrus Dressing:
1 tbsp honey
2 tbsps olive oil
1 whole lemon, zested and juiced
¼ cup orange juice

Assembly Directions:

1) Make the dressing by mixing all dressing ingredients in a bowl thoroughly. Evenly divide into 4 servings and pour into Mason jars.
2) To assemble fruit salad, divide each fruit into 4 servings and layer in this sequence: blackberries, strawberries, blueberries and almonds.
3) Cover and refrigerate. Consume within 2 days of preparation.

California Roll in a Jar

Servings: 1 1-pint Mason jar

Ingredients:
½ cup cooked white rice, hot
¼ cup chopped cucumber
1 sheet nori, cut into 1-inch long strips
4 pieces imitation crab sticks, thawed and chopped roughly
½ avocado, sliced into strips
¼ tsp salt
1 tsp rice vinegar
½ tsp sugar
2 tbsps Kewpie mayonnaise
1 tsp lemon juice

Assembly Directions:

1) In a small bowl, mix sugar, salt and rice vinegar. Once white rice is cooked, measure ½ cup and place into bowl of rice vinegar mixture. Toss to coat and mix well. Allow to cool completely.
2) In a bowl, toss together avocado and lemon juice. This will prevent discoloration of avocado.
3) To assemble California roll, layer ingredients in the following sequence: Rice, mayonnaise, cucumber, crab sticks, nori, and avocado.

4) Cover and refrigerate. Consume within 2 days of preparation.

Garlic-Lemon Tahini Dressing on Beet & Quinoa Salad

Servings: 1 1-quart Mason jar

Ingredients:
2 cups spinach
1 tbsp sunflower seeds
¼ cup smoked tofu extra firm, chopped
½ cup cooked quinoa
¼ cup shredded beets
1 cup chickpeas, rinsed and drained well
½ cup shredded carrots
2 tbsps dressing

Garlic-Lemon Tahini Dressing Ingredients:
Pepper and salt to taste
¼ cup water
2 minced garlic cloves
2 tbsps olive oil
3 tbsps tahini
1 lemon, juiced

Assembly Directions:

1) In food processor, place all dressing ingredients
   and process until smooth and creamy. Add 2 tbsps

of dressing into Mason jar and store remaining dressing for future use.

2) To assemble salad in jar, layer ingredients in the following order: dressing, carrots, chickpeas, beets, quinoa and spinach.

3) Cover and refrigerate. Consume within 5 days of making.

Basil-Raspberry Vinaigrette on Spring Cobb

Servings: 1 1-quart Mason jar

Ingredients:
4 cups fresh spinach
4 bacon strips, cooked to a crisp and diced
¾ cup fresh raspberries
3 hard-boiled eggs, chopped
3 medium sized tomatoes, diced finely
½ large cucumber, diced finely
1 large chicken breast
Pepper and salt to taste
½ tsp garlic powder

Basil-Raspberry Vinaigrette Ingredients:
¼ tsp salt
2 tbsps honey
½ cup fresh raspberries
1 tsp dried basil
¼ cup red wine vinegar
¾ cup olive oil

Assembly Directions:

1) Season chicken breast with garlic powder, salt and pepper. Grill on medium fire for 6 minutes per side or until chicken is cooked and juices run clear.

Transfer cooked chicken to chopping board and allow to cool completely. Once cooled, chopped chicken to ½-inch cubes.

2) In food processor, combine all vinaigrette ingredients and puree until smooth and creamy. Scoop out 2 tbsps of dressing into Mason jar and store remaining dressing for future use.

3) To assemble salad, layer ingredients in the following order: cucumber, tomatoes, raspberries, chicken, 2 cups spinach, hard boiled eggs, diced bacon and remaining spinach.

4) Cover and refrigerate. Consume within 2 days of making.

Chicken Salad Sriracha Flavor

Servings: 2 1-quart Mason jar

Ingredients:
Pepper and salt to taste
2 chicken breast, boneless and skinless
Juice from 1 lime
1 garlic clove, minced
2 tbsps Sriracha sauce
½ tsp molasses
½ tsp balsamic vinegar
1 tbsp fish sauce
½ cup fresh pineapple chunks
4 cups baby spinach
½ cup fresh pineapple chunks
1 cup cherry tomatoes, halved
½ cup diced red onion
1 avocado, cubed

Dressing Ingredients:
3 tbsps extra virgin olive oil
1 garlic clove, minced
1 lime, juiced and zested
1 tbsp raw honey
1 tbsp Sriracha sauce
2 tsps Dijon mustard

Assembly Directions:

1) In a zip lock bag, place chicken. Add pepper and salt to taste. Mix in lime juice, garlic, sriracha, molasses, balsamic vinegar, fish sauce and pineapple chunks. Seal bag and mix well. Place chicken in the ref to marinate for at least an hour.
2) Grill chicken on medium fire for 6 minutes per side or until chicken is cooked and juices run clear. Transfer chicken to chopping board and cool completely. Chop into ½-inch cubes.
3) In food processor, process all dressing ingredients until smooth and creamy. Evenly divide into 2 Mason jars.
4) To assemble salad, divide ingredients into two and layer following this sequence: avocados, tomatoes, pineapple, chicken and spinach.
5) Cover and refrigerate. Consume within 2 days of making.

Caprese and Pasta Salad in a Jar

Servings: 1 1-pint Mason jar

Ingredients:
½ cup fresh basil, chopped
½ cup fresh spinach
2 oz cooked penne pasta
1 ½ oz fresh mozzarella, chopped into bite sized pieces
1 cup cherry tomatoes
2 tbsps basil pesto

Assembly Directions:

1) To assemble, layer the following ingredients in order: pesto, mozzarella, tomatoes, penne pasta, chopped basil and spinach.
2) Cover and refrigerate. Consume within 3 days of making.

Greek Pasta Salad with Lemon Vinaigrette

Servings: 1 1-pint Mason jar

Ingredients:
½ cup fresh mint, chopped
½ cup mixed greens
2 oz rigatoni, cooked
½ cup feta, crumbled
1 cup cucumber, chopped
¼ cup red onion, chopped
1 cup cherry tomatoes
2 tbsps lemon vinaigrette

Lemon Vinaigrette Ingredients:
A couple of grinds of black pepper
A good pinch of salt
½ cup olive oil
Juice from one lemon

Assembly Directions:

1) In a lidded container, mix all vinaigrette ingredients and shake vigorously. Scoop out 2 tbsps of vinaigrette and pour into Mason jar.
2) To assemble salad, layer the ingredients in the following order: tomatoes, cucumber, onions, pasta, cheese, mint and mixed greens.

3) Cover and refrigerate. Consume within 3 days of making.

Carrot Noodle Salad

Servings: 2 1-pint Mason jars

Ingredients:
2 cups spinach
1/3 cup cashews
2 tbsps Bob's Red Mill hulled hemp seeds
1 roasted bell pepper, chopped
2 carrots spiralized
1 tbsp toasted sesame seeds
1 tsp Dark Amber maple syrup
1 tsp soy sauce
1 tsp rice vinegar
½ tsp garlic powder
1 tbsp Thai sweet red chili sauce
1 tbsp toasted sesame oil

Assembly Directions:

1) In a bowl, mix well sesame seeds, maple syrup, soy sauce, vinegar, garlic powder, sweet red chili sauce and sesame oil. Evenly divide into 2 Mason jars.
2) To assemble salad, divide all ingredients equally in two and layer in the following sequence: carrot noodles, bell pepper, hemp seeds, cashews and spinach.

3) Cover and refrigerate. Consume within 5 days of making.

Poppy-Citrus Dressing on Spinach-Strawberry Salad

Servings: 2 1-quart Mason jars

Ingredients:
2 tbsps sliced almonds, toasted
1 5-oz bag of Spinach
8 oz grilled skinless chicken breast
¼ avocado, chopped
½ cup roasted asparagus chopped
4 large strawberries, chopped
½ cup cucumber slices
¼ cup red onion slices
6 tbsps Poppy-citrus Dressing

Poppy-Citrus Dressing Ingredients:
1 ½ tbsps olive oil
1 tsp poppy seeds
1 clove garlic, minced
1 tsp Dijon mustard
¼ tsp ground pepper
½ tsp salt
1 tbsp maple syrup
½ cup fresh grapefruit juice

Assembly Directions:

1) In food processor, combine all dressing ingredients and puree until smooth and creamy. Scoop out 3 tbsps of dressing and pour into two Mason jars.

2) To assemble salad in jar and layer in the following sequence: ½ of onions, ½ of cucumbers, ½ of strawberries, ½ of asparagus, ½ of chicken, ½ of avocado, ½ of spinach and ½ of almonds.

3) Cover and refrigerate. Eat within 2 days of making.

Conclusion

So, now that you have lots of ideas on how to create a Mason jar salad, I wish you the best of luck on your road to a healthier lifestyle. Remember that the key to keeping your salads in a jar fresh is to make sure that the ingredients that you put in are quite dry. For example, lettuce and spinach leaves would last longer if after washing, remove the excess water through a salad spinner or patting dry with a paper towel.

Also, the next rule to remember in order to keep your salads in a jar fresher for a longer period is to place the wet ingredients at the bottom of the jar. Adding pasta, rice, quinoa, bulgur and other in the layer would absorb the moisture from the wet ingredients keeping your green leaves crunchier and will make it last longer.

I hope that you will have a great time and enjoy the different Mason jar salad recipes that I have prepared for you.

Made in United States
Troutdale, OR
05/04/2025

31111789R00056